Yankee
Go Home

Yankee Go Home

Dr. Phil Maymin

Also by the author

Yankee Wake Up

Free Your Inner Yankee

NBA Mysticism: Prophecies Fulfilled and Fortunes Told

---

philmaymin.com | phil@maymin.com

ISBN: 1460938674
ISBN-13:   978-1460938676

The cover art is from Wikimedia Commons:

```
http://commons.wikimedia.org/wiki/File:Yankees_
        kicking_out_the_British.jpg
```

Its description reads: "1890's caricature of Americans kicking out the British. Uncle Sam looks on as a youthful George Washington in tricorne hat kicks John Bull across the water."

Sometimes the only way a Yankee can come home is if no one else is in it. In this picture, Yankees are clearing their home of tyranny. Not a bad practice to get into.

Printed in the United States of America.

Dedication and Acknowledgements

This book is dedicated to my family.

I am grateful to my editor Nick Keppler at *Fairfield County Weekly,* where almost all of these articles first appeared, and to Josh Mamis, the publisher.

I am also grateful to Lew Rockwell, who republished several of these articles at lewrockwell.com.

Table of Contents

INTRODUCTION

Yankee, this is my home.

Yankees are believers in liberty, Americans, rugged and hardy individuals. When foreigners shout "Yankee Go Home," they protest being occupied by American forces. But what does it mean when an American shouts it? What does it mean when one Yankee tells another to go home?

It means: people of America, return to America. Return to your roots of freedom and limited government and no entangling foreign alliances. Bring the Yankee troops back, bring the Yankee money used as foreign aid back, bring the Yankee values back.

For me in this book, it also has a more personal meaning. In 2006 when I ran for the U.S. House of Representatives, just about every newspaper in the area ran numerous stories and interviews with me. All except one: *The Fairfield County Weekly*.

The editor at the time, Tom Gogola, tried several times to arrange something, but things kept coming up. After the election, Tom apologized and invited me to submit an article. I did. Then another one. Before I knew it, 4.5 years had gone by. This volume is the last of the collection of my articles. As of February 2011, because of time constraints and changing circumstances, I have decided to stop writing for them to focus more on my own fundamental work in other fields.

I am a Yankee and I am going home.

Bye!

Phil Maymin, February 2011

FREEDOM TO FORNICATE

When it comes to sex, we are all libertarians. Why aren't we on all issues of personal freedom?

On any other matter, people largely divide into left and right camps, each trying to legislate their own morality, but if you look at the two major government parties, you would think that nobody believes speech should be as free as sex.

The left wants to censor anti-environmentalists and the right wants to censor anti-imperialists. Speech is okay so long as it is pre-approved by those in power. We can't allow racist speech or hate speech or unpatriotic speech. Commerce and trade is even more regulated.

But not sex. Even the most heavy-handed politicians on either side of the aisle wouldn't dare directly regulate sex. It may be our last free act.

You can have sex with whoever you want. Of course, it's not the lawlessness of anarchy, but the justice of libertarianism: Do what you like as long as you don't harm others. You can't have sex with people who don't want to have sex with you, or who don't have the capacity to agree to it. And you can't have unprotected sex with people if you knowingly carry a deadly disease. That would be murder. But otherwise, rock on.

You can discriminate with your partners. There are no equal opportunity statutes for sex. You can discriminate on the basis of gender or race or religion or age or nationality or sexual preference or even political beliefs. Only want to sleep with tall, blonde, lesbian Swedish libertarians? Go ahead. No one will arrest you, ticket you or torture you. Just don't try discriminating with speech or trade. Both government parties will denounce you as a villain.

You can boast as much as you want about your prowess. Are you the world's greatest lover? There is no federal agency that will review your claim, and no one for your partners to complain to if they disagree. There is no penalty for being inefficient and no subsidy for environmentally friendly sex. But try running a campaign ad without explicitly approving your own message at the end. Try selling a toilet that flushes instead of drizzles. Try hanging on to your non-green-starred incandescent bulbs. That would be evil!

You don't need to fill out any forms to have sex. There is no licensing requirement. There are no approved or unapproved sexual procedures. There is no department you have to wait in line and register with, no mandatory exams, no federal agency certifying safety and efficiency, not even a standardized aptitude test. But try starting a company without putting up harassment posters and paying unemployment insurance. Try offering medical or legal or electrical or plumbing advice to your friends. It's the fast track to jail.

You can even have babies nine months later. You can create life without any form of government approval, but you can't issue your own currency. You can have twins and octuplets, but you can't opt out of killing innocent Iraqis and Afghanis. You can grow a miracle in your belly, but you can't keep your earned money or owned property without paying taxes on each.

If the left and right did try to legislate sex, they would be laughed out of town. We would suggest to our elected officers in quite graphic terms what sexual activity they could do to each other instead.

But there is no such indignation when they tell us which doctors we can see, what loans we can make, what businesses we can start, what citizens of foreign countries we can support.

We wouldn't stand for sex insurance for the unattractive or sexual social security for the elderly or sexcaid for the poor. If you are a sexual libertarian — and most people are — then you should be a libertarian about every other policy issue as well.

Otherwise, we are just choosing which particular politician, the one on the left or the one on the right, will be the next to screw us.

Originally published on January 21, 2010

FALSE VICTORY

Obama has a "mission accomplished" moment in the war on the economy

Nearly seven years ago, President Bush stood on the flight deck of a warship and declared victory in Iraq. "My fellow Americans," Bush said, "major combat operations in Iraq have ended." A "mission accomplished" banner infamously hung in the background.

It turned out, of course, that we had barely begun murdering Iraqis and sacrificing Americans.

Last week, President Obama addressed the nation and proudly declared victory on the economy. Insisting that he had acted "immediately and aggressively" to avert a second depression, Obama proclaimed, "The worst of the storm has passed."

Uh-oh. Does this mean we have only scratched the surface in terms of government interventions, bailouts, and back-room deals to "rescue" the market?

Unfortunately, yes. When the next big crash happens, the administration will not admit it was wrong to overregulate the economy. It will not even admit its various bills and acts failed, let alone caused the collapse. Instead, we will be told that greedy bankers and selfish managers have intentionally decreased productivity, and this unpatriotic stewardship of our financial system will not stand. We will be told that what we need is even more regulation and centralized control.

The reason we didn't withdraw from Iraq then, and the reason we won't withdraw from the market now, is the same. Politicians can't give up their illusion of control.

Nobody wants to go down in history as overseeing a military or economic loss, and it is impossible to know what would have happened had the president done nothing, or even the exact opposite, so any gains can be chalked up to good leadership and any losses to bad luck. (This is a psychological effect called the self-serving bias.)

If not for his activity, Obama claimed, "unemployment might be double what it is today." Might be; it also could be half.

"More businesses would certainly have closed." Like AIG and GM? Then perhaps more businesses should have closed.

"More homes would have surely been lost." Lost to what? The houses themselves would be fine. Their prices would have declined, and banks would have had to take write-offs. Then, working taxpayers with some savings would have been able to afford a house. Instead, they rent and pay taxes so that someone who paid too much for a house can keep it at an inflated price, maintaining a steady stream of interest payments to the banks and government entities like Fannie Mae and Freddie Mac.

As little justification as the government had to intervene in Iraq, it has even less to intervene in the markets. We could withdraw our military and economic troops from both at any time. Indeed, Obama promises to have zero combat troops in Iraq by the end of August. (We will see if it actually happens.) There is no loss of face for him in Iraq, but there is in the market.

So how much has Obama just cost us? We can actually calculate it. The "worst of the storm" happened last year when the market was 35 percent lower than it is today. Assuming that the implicit guarantee is in place at least until the 2012 election, we can price the value of the option Obama sold with his State of the Union address. In the language of equity derivatives, Obama sold a 33-month, 35 percent out-of-the-money put option on the market capitalization of the entire world.

Obama's gaffe options are probably worth more than $2 trillion dollars in present value, even if the market never does fall again. That means that if Obama had sold them in the free market, investors would have paid several trillion dollars for a guarantee that the worst really was behind us. Of course, Obama sold it out for nothing, for zero. He sold us out for a self-congratulatory soundbite.

And that's not all. The trillions in lost revenue are just the present value of the option. If the market actually does fall, Obama has signed a blank check with your name on it.

Originally published on February 4, 2010

NUREMBERG ODDS

Chances are slim Obama will give accused terrorists the kind of trials the World War II powers gave the Nazis

After World War II, the victorious nations negotiated amongst themselves how to try the leaders of Nazi Germany. They settled on military tribunals held in Nuremberg. The U.S., Britain, the Soviet Union and France each provided one judge, one alternate and one prosecutor. German lawyers acted as defense attorneys. Twenty-two high-ranking Nazi leaders were tried.

Only 12 were sentenced to death, and only three others got a life sentence. Of the remaining seven, four got jail sentences ranging from 10 to 20 years, and three were acquitted outright.

Would we be comfortable with those odds for the alleged terrorists behind 9/11? We have charged five people with the murder of 2,973 victims, with terrorism and other associated crimes. Would we be comfortable if the Nuremberg ratios applied here? That would mean only two would be executed. One more would get a life sentence. Another would only be sentenced to a decade or two in jail. One would be acquitted outright.

Karl Dönitz was the commander of the German navy and was named by Hitler to be his successor. He was convicted of war crimes and sentenced to a decade in jail. In 1956, he was released, and lived another 24 years before a fatal heart attack. Hitler's Minister of Armaments and War Production, Albert

Speer, was only sentenced to 20 years for using slave labor, because he expressed repentance. He was released in 1966 and died in 1981.

Would we be comfortable if Khalid Sheikh Mohammed got that kind of sentence? Imagine the reaction of the American people. Imagine your reaction.

We can't blame President Barack Obama's administration if he wants to establish, beyond a reasonable doubt, that the people they execute did, in fact, commit the acts they are executed for. Indeed, what would be the alternative? Unilateral death sentences by the executive branch, with no appeal, defense or review? So if Obama wants to convince objective, dispassionate people in a fair trial that these five were ultimately responsible for the deaths of 2,973 people, so be it.

But a fair trial may not be what he wants. A fair trial carries with it a chance of error. Innocent people die and guilty people go free. We try to minimize both errors, but punishing the innocent is worse, so we build in many checks and balances. We presume innocence and require proof of guilt. The rules of evidence typically do not allow inappropriately gathered facts or coerced confessions. As Homer Simpson exclaimed after his mother got sent to jail on a technicality, "People should only get sent out of jail on technicalities!" And he's right. That's why technicalities exist.

How would we feel if the mastermind of the 9/11 attacks got off on a technicality? How would Obama look? Do you honestly think that the man who has unconstitutionally overturned the automobile, financial and medical industries, the man who now claims he can examine your cell phone location without a warrant, will allow any justice system to come to a conclusion other than five deaths? His press secretary Robert Gibbs declared on CNN recently that Khalid Sheikh Mohammed "will be brought to justice, and he's likely to be executed for the heinous crimes he committed."

All the terrorists' defense needs to do is raise a reasonable doubt. According to polls, about a third of Americans suspect that 9/11 was "an inside job." Considering that, we'd be lucky to get a single execution. After all, the death penalty requires unanimous agreement by the commission judges.

But that's not the scary part. The scary part will be when Obama somehow, through backroom deals or outright intervention, overturns the results of an independent judiciary. Then, with our economy, society and justice system totally controlled by one man, the terrorists will have won.

My advice to Obama? Do not get involved. Stay away, because this is not your domain. Let the justice system work and hope that it does, but know that if we corrupt it, we do far more damage than an imprisoned terrorist could ever do.

Given Obama's policies on GM, AIG, TARP, Iraq, Afghanistan, health care and the environment, it seems staying away isn't his thing. Total and unilateral control is.

Originally published on February 18, 2010

FAILING AT FREEDOM

Barack Obama is not a libertarian.
He couldn't even recognize one.

President Barack Obama addressed the Business Roundtable last week to deny allegations of socialism and to proclaim his "ardent belief in free markets."

Has he become a libertarian? Surely, Obama is not a libertarian on foreign policy. The Nobel Peace Prize-winner still wants to keep our troops on other countries' soil fighting other people's battles. Just as surely he is not a libertarian on social and civil issues. He saved the Patriot Act from expiration last week. He supports warrantless surveillance on phone calls. He laughs off questions about the legalization of drugs. He doesn't even pretend to be a libertarian on health care. He would never allow you to opt out of insurance or allow you to decide what treatments are effective for you. And don't even think about starting a business without paying for health insurance for your employees.

But maybe Obama has recently become a libertarian on economic issues. In his speech, he referred directly to the recent surge of libertarianism in America, citing the rise in anti-government feeling. He used the words "anger" and "frustration" nine times in a single paragraph.

Some of the pro-freedom sentiment goes under the "tea party" moniker. Much of it is due to Ron Paul's influence. But the vast bulk is not an organized movement. It is just millions of ticked off Americans. There is no hierarchical structure with a single leader on top. But Obama cannot fathom anything like that. He thinks he is speaking at least obliquely to the people who "lead" the freedom movement.

He is way off. The Business Roundtable is not a libertarian organization, nor does it speak for any libertarians that I am aware of. While there are numerous legitimate organizations of businesses, most large organizations are barely disguised lobby groups. This same Business Roundtable supported Obama's Recovery Act. Who are they to opine on matters of economic freedom?

Nevertheless, Obama carries on, revealing his total miscomprehension of the basic elements of freedom and liberty. His biggest misunderstanding: He thinks liberty is all about agreeing. How did America achieve "global leadership" in the last century? "[B]y working together to define our destiny and seize the future," he said. And to do it in this century, we must "summon that same resolve." He thinks we can have a thriving America again only if we "move forward as one nation." We must "all pick up an oar and start rowing in the same direction."

The idea that freedom means agreement sounds reasonable at first blush. Indeed, contracts and voluntary exchange are prime indicators of a free country. But freedom and liberty actually prosper through disagreement. Progress and wealth creation comes about because people have different goals. Think of trading volume on stocks. If everybody agreed, there would be no volume. Who would you trade with? Contracts and exchanges occur precisely because people disagree. I value your time more than I value my money; you feel the opposite, so we trade and are both better off.

That is Obama's fundamental flaw. Revising history in a Marxian way, he argues that "throughout history" government has fostered "sustained economic growth." That's absurd. Economic growth is just a measure, like trading volume, of how much people disagree. Sustained economic growth is like sustained trading volume — it can't be imposed by force.

Obama praises his beloved social redistribution programs for helping "secure broad-based consensus that is so critical to a functioning market economy." He fails to understand that consensus kills freedom and market economies, especially when enforced by government.

Obama is not a libertarian (on any issue). But the people increasingly are, and Obama sees the writing on the wall and he is scared. Americans are not angry and frustrated because we want a different consensus. We want no consensus at all. We want to be free to disagree.

Originally published on March 4, 2010

THE ISRAELI LIBERTARIANS

A small movement for freedom begins in one of the most statist countries on the planet

With Tea Parties all around us, President Obama's approval at all-time lows and dissatisfaction with government seemingly ubiquitous, you might wonder if this kind of discontent is happening in other countries.

In Israel, one of the world's longest-lasting bastions of socialism and concentrated state power, the flower of liberty has not yet started to bloom, but seeds are afoot. Boris Karpa, a graduate student of history at Tel Aviv University, is spearheading a libertarian uprising. His Israeli freedom blog is at www.libertarian.org.il. Karpa agreed to an exclusive interview with the *Weekly*.

Phil Maymin: What is your position? Are you the unofficial head and founder of the Israeli libertarian movement?

Boris Karpa: You can call me that, but I do not formally claim any such title, because Israel has had libertarians and libertarian movements before me, and we have several think tanks. Technically, I founded the Facebook group and the activist group in general. I certainly am the admin of the group. I also founded and administer the Tel Aviv University Students for Liberty.

What is the history of libertarianism in Israel?

In general, libertarianism and market liberalism is not a big part of Israel's history. Aside from an abortive anti-tax party in the 1970s and similar such marginal attempts, there's precious few libertarian activists in this country. There are several think tanks, however, that do great work promoting libertarian ideas, especially libertarian economics, through seminars, press releases and so forth. I must especially commend the Jerusalem Institute of Market Studies, who focus on the promotion of Austrian economic thought.

Why is it do you think that Jews and libertarianism don't get along? I would have thought the pair would be a perfect match, with the shared focus on law and justice and freedom. Next week is Passover, the Jewish festival celebrating their exodus from slavery, one of the most libertarian holidays anywhere.

I think that the main issue is that, when you look back to the history of zionism, it didn't grow up in a vacuum. Zionism was inspired greatly by the nationalist movements of Europe, and these movements were very influenced by socialism and collectivism. So the principal idea of classical zionism, which is what the dominant strain of zionism was called, was that the Jewish state must be socialist in some way. And that the capitalist, bourgeois life of European Jews — who as you know often tended to work as attorneys and engineers and white-collar bourgeois types — was a form of moral corruption. Therefore, the zionists felt they had to focus on creating something they called "The New Jew." We're talking about the leading faction of zionists here, the people who later held power in Israel for its first few decades. And so the New Jew had to be re-accustomed to manual labor. That's part of why the Kibbutzim were created. The idea was to take this stereotypical Jewish attorney and make him into a hard-working farmer — a socialist, hard-working farmer.

That's disgusting. I never realized that.

And of course they realized not everybody could be farmers. But the thing you need to understand about early Israel is that it was led by very statist people.

This might be a difference between our countries. Americans are at heart very libertarian. They deeply believe in freedom and distrust government. Do you feel Israelis, at heart, are also freedom loving people or do you feel Israelis are really and truly statist, meaning your road is much harder than ours?

I think our job would be harder, to some extent, than yours is, because Americans can fall back on the inspiration of people like Thomas Jefferson, who were not libertarians, perhaps, but who were anti-statist and understood the dangers of an out-of-control government. For us, these founder figures we look up to are people like Ben Gurion. But I think the average Israeli realizes at some level how high the taxes are, how crazy the bureaucracy is, that he's lost freedoms and money to the ever-growing state.

But there are far older heroes for Jews. Do you think there are libertarians in the Old Testament? Who is the most libertarian?

Samuel, definitely Samuel, he's the most libertarian guy. … [I]f you recall, originally, the Jews had no king. Their religious life was administered by the priests who also led them in battle, and some form of wise men they respected served as judges locally. The only police we have in the Bible are fellows who enforced order on the temple grounds. But at a certain point, the Jews decide that they want a king. And if the Bible is to be believed, Samuel gives a long speech warning them about all the evils a king can do — about the king taking a tenth of their income in taxes and drafting their sons to ride his chariots and his daughters to be his slavegirls. He goes on and on in this vein. You know, when the Israeli Center for Social and Economic Progress printed Milton Friedman's Free to Choose in Hebrew, they printed Samuel's speech on the front page.

What is the biggest problem in Israel? What argument for liberty resonates the most with people?

I think the main problem in Israel is the bureaucracy. You see, government in Israel operates in a vastly different principle from American government. The U.S. has several levels of legislature, and when they want to make a new law, they pass a bill of 1,500 pages because they want to leave as little as possible to the bureaucrats. Here we have one legislature and some city councils that are virtually powerless. And the legislature passes a bill of 20 pages which creates bureaucrats, and they create regulations as they see fit. And so there's an enormous army of bureaucrats in every level of government making rules and determinations and licenses, which every citizen must contend with if they want to do something.

Well, we also have tons of agencies, like the SEC, FDA, EPA, etc., who create their own rules, but you're saying there's something even more?

Absolutely. Because the rules are made by appointees. For example, we have the Beach Protection Council.

Sounds sexy.

If you want to have a new development on a beach, then after going through all the regular planning hoops, you must also get the council's approval. And because their job, as they see it, is to protect beaches from those nasty developers. ... Bottom line, the council measures its success in how many applications it denied. ... Another example: The government made motor racing legal several years ago. But they made it conditional on a committee making up some safety regulations and so forth. And because the committee is still working on it, we still can't have motor sports in this country. Can you imagine what would happen if Congress banned NASCAR?

Originally published on March 18, 2010

WAITING FOR SANANDA

The government is one giant cult

In 1954, Dorothy Martin, a Chicago housewife, announced she had been receiving messages from outer space telling her the Western Hemisphere would be destroyed by a flood on Dec. 21. The messages came from a being called Sananda, who assured Dorothy the true believers would be rescued by a flying saucer just before midnight the night before the flood. Dorothy first tried to get the word out to save as many people as possible, but in September, her small group, called the "Seekers," shut down all outside communications. Many quit their jobs, left their spouses and gave away their money and possessions. Per Sananda's instructions, they removed all metal from their clothes.

On Dec. 20, 20 or so people crowded into Dorothy's home to await Sananda. The clock struck midnight. No visitor. One Seeker noticed a second clock showed only 11:55 p.m. The Seekers reached a consensus that it was not yet midnight.

When even the slow clock showed 12:10 a.m., one guy put on his hat and went home. Perhaps he thought he could get his job and wife back. The rest stayed, in stunned silence.

A little after 4 a.m., Dorothy got another message. The disaster had been called off. The little group, sitting all night long, had spread so much light that God saved the world from destruction.

The next afternoon, the group called newspapers, friends, anybody who will listen, to spread their message. Their single, most important prediction had proven blindingly obviously false, but their reaction was renewed vigor and belief.

Sound familiar? For 50 years, our government dispersed our military to every corner of the globe, whether the locals wanted us there or not. Resentment grew, and that resentment grew into a movement. One of its results was the hideous terrorist attack on 9/11, in clear retaliation to our unjustified imperialism. What was our response? More troops to countries entirely unaffiliated with the 9/11 attackers.

For almost a century, our government has controlled the value of money through the central bank. Inflation has ravished the dollar. Regulations and guarantees only encouraged reckless risks. In the Great Depression, much as in the past few years, the mistakes of centralized economic planning became obvious. What was our response? More centralized economic planning.

A few years ago, a campaign called Earth Hour started with feeble support. The intent was to have people switch off electricity in their homes and businesses to make a point about the environment. In the last year, global warming has been shown to be fraudulent and simply wrong, as proof came that scientists essentially fabricated evidence. It's clear the effects of humans on the environment is negligible. But Earth Hour founder Andy Ridley said recently the movement has only grown. The environmentalists reacted just as the cult did to the exposé of the myth: spread the word. This year, a thousand landmarks and the offices of many global companies across 300,000 cities in over 100 countries darkened for Earth Hour.

Why does this happen? We actually know why, because three psychologists infiltrated the Seekers, testing what was then a new theory of cognitive dissonance, that uncomfortable feeling you get from holding conflicting ideas. The psychologists predicted that when the aliens failed to come, those who had invested the most in being rescued would strengthen their resolve.

Five conditions must be met for someone to become a more fervent believer after disconfirmation. First, the belief must be held with deep conviction. Second, the person must have made substantial commitment, the more irreversible the better. Third, the belief must be such that events could refute it. Fourth, the undeniable evidence must occur. And fifth, most importantly, the person must know others who support the idea.

Fanatics can't be reasoned with. If our government is like Dorothy, we are in trouble; even though the rest of the cult eventually dispersed, she continued to act as a channel for Sananda until her death. But perhaps we can draw inspiration from her husband. He never supported Dorothy's visions. On the eve before the cataclysm, he slept soundly through the night.

Originally published on March 31, 2010

BLOODY TAXES

If you support forced redistribution of wealth, you should also support forced redistribution of blood

edistribution means taking from some to give to others. But from whom, and in what proportion? And to whom, and in what proportion? How much? These are incredibly obvious questions but nobody asks them, let alone answer them. Why not? For two different reasons.

Those who support redistribution tend not to ask or allow others to ask basic questions about it, out of feelings of guilt and shame. Redistribution needs to be believed in and if you question it in any way there must be something wrong with you.

Those who oppose redistribution simply view it as stealing, and asking these questions is akin to asking what optimal amount of mugging should be tolerated in a city. It's repugnant.

But let's you and I think about it a little bit, on this April 15th day of taxes and spending. Most of the federal budget is spent on redistribution in various forms: Social Security, Medicare and Medicaid, food stamps, housing assistance, and many more. Let's be a little abstract so that we can distance ourselves both from the guilt and the repugnance that quashes our natural curiosity. Let's ask some basic questions.

How much money should be redistributed from the wealthy to the poor? Is it a fixed number that depends on the needs of the poor, or is it a variable number that depends on the profits of the wealthy? What does it mean to be wealthy, high recent income or lifetime accumulated assets?

How should the largess be distributed? Equally to everyone below a certain threshold? Should those who are poorer receive more? What does it mean to be poor, low recent income or lifetime accumulated debt?

How often should the redistribution took place? Once, to account for past injustices, or repeatedly, like clockwork?

Most importantly, how can we objectively think about these questions without resorting to character accusations?

One approach is to proceed by analogy. Start with your body. Just about everybody has extra blood. By all of the standard arguments for redistribution – need, excess wealth, not the result of hard work, fairness – blood should be redistributed. Along with your 1040, you should send along a baggie of blood. Should everybody be forced to redistribute blood?

People need blood. According to America's Blood Centers, someone needs blood every two seconds. One in seven people entering a hospital will need blood. One pint of blood can save up to three lives. Here, the redistribution questions are easy: everybody who needs blood for medical reasons should get all that they need, whenever they need it.

Only a small minority have the appropriate blood. Only 38 percent of the U.S. population is eligible. And everybody in that blood-wealthy group can spare a little. The amount of blood to be redistributed depends only on the amount needed to save people, not on the amount the donors can spare.

Your blood type is not the result of hard work or ingenuity. Taking some of your blood, unlike taking some of your money, won't affect your incentive to work. Therefore, we could redistribute this repeatedly.

It is only fair that those who have better blood through no credit of their own and who could safely give some of it up, be forced to do so, to redistribute it to those who need blood through no fault of their own and whose lives could be saved.

Blood is better than money because politicians can't even pocket any. All of it goes to the intended recipients.

Do you support forced redistribution of money? Do you support forced redistribution of blood? If your answers to the two questions are not the same, you have a problem on your hands.

Originally published on April 15, 2010

THE WAR ON RISK
Obama wants to end chance itself

America's wars have become increasingly abstract. First we fought the British. Then we fought ourselves. Then the Germans. Then the Germans and Japanese. Then the Koreans and Vietnamese. Somewhere along the way we found non-human enemies. We started fighting drugs. At least that was still alive, albeit in the vegetable kingdom. But then we declared war on poverty, an economic condition. Then terror, a contingent emotion. Now we have declared our final war against risk itself.

If we win this war, then we will have won all wars. No enemy would be able to take us by surprise. Terror would be a thing of the past, generating academic curiosity and smug contempt, much like slavery does now. We will shake our heads and wonder how people could possibly have lived like that when there was this better way.

Illegal drug use would be out of the question and all approved drugs would have no random side effects. Life would be nice and steady. Our economy would grow at a constant two percent per year. The options markets would be shut down and the stock market would be replaced with a chalkboard since all stock prices would merely grow at the same rate as the economy.

We would never have another bubble, in any assets, ever again. We would never have any car accidents or delayed flights or natural disasters. We would have tamed risk, and the universe itself. Electrons would no longer randomly and bizarrely live in a probabilistic world: Heisenberg's uncertainty principle would be outlawed and we would know the exact position and momentum of every single particle in the universe.

Innovation and creativity do not have to wither and die. They could be managed and expected. It sounds like fantasy but it is not really that outlandish. Creative people constantly develop brand new ideas on a deadline. We will, as a society, plan our future inventions. The patent office would be able to predict future products and issue pre-emptive patents. Most importantly, financial crises will be a thing of the past.

Last week, President Obama launched the opening salvo in our new war against risk with a specific, 89-page description of financial reform. Financial firms would be more regulated so they could never again fail. Financial markets would be more transparent so they could never again cause losses. Consumers and investors would have government protection. The government would have a broad range of new powers, of course, because after all, this is war. And the international community would be organized into a community with a common enemy: the unknown.

Obama praised his own proposal as being "by all accounts... a commonsense, reasonable, non-ideological approach."

Well, he was already wrong on one thing. It is not "by all accounts." Hi there! I disagree.

My father and I recently proved in a research article that any regulation of risk actually increases risk. Moreover, any objective regulatory algorithm to measure and manage risk capital will always result in independent banks simultaneously choosing to invest in securities that appear to be low risk based on the particular algorithm, but which in fact have higher risk. We proved this both mathematically and empirically, and it holds for any regulation where the measure of risk is objective. In other words, Obama's proposal is doomed to fail. What's worse is that the introduction of new regulations will only increase the probability and severity of future financial crises.

Does that mean we are doomed to a life of chaos? That risk itself has won?

There are two ways out of the risk-increasing regulatory morass, and they both work by making risk management a subjective rather than an objective process. One way is to fully nationalize all financial firms. We can then just focus on finding good quality regulators to run them. They will be able to make subjective decisions about each bank's portfolio and lending decisions without the handcuffs of an objective rule. Perhaps this is Obama's ultimate goal. But of course then risk does not disappear but merely lie in wait as economic and financial decisions get made for political purposes, and any tiny loss can become a collapse of the entire system, since they are all integrated.

The only other possible solution is a complete deregulation of all financial entities. That would mean shutting down the Federal Reserve, America's central bank. It would also mean ending the FDIC, federal deposit insurance. When you put money in a bank, you would have to be confident in that bank, just like when you invest money in a stock, you have to be confident in that stock. After all, a bank is nothing more than a company that takes your money, hands out long term loans, and tries repay you on demand.

This is not as radical as it seems. Indeed, perhaps counterintuitively, allowing risk to reign free would reduce risk. In a free market, when a bank fails, only that bank fails, and at worst a handful of others who depended on it to their detriment. The system remains. The possibility of a financial crisis lessens.

We have tried the approach that has been billed as commonsense and middle-of-the-road. We may disagree whether we should veer off the cliff to full nationalization or pull over to complete deregulation, but one thing is clear: when you are fighting against risk, the one place you don't want to be left standing is in the middle of the road.

Originally published on April 29, 2010

ELECTION OF THE BODY SNATCHERS!

A proposed New York State law could tighten government's grip on your body

Who owns your body? Those organs sloshing around inside you — who do they belong to?

New York Assemblyman Richard Brodsky (D-Westchester County), a candidate for the office of New York attorney general, has recently proposed a law to mandate organ donation, subject to some ability to opt out. I learned of his proposal just a few weeks after my article in this space pointing out that forced redistribution of wealth is on the same moral level as forced redistribution of blood ("Bloody Taxes," April 15). Many readers wrote to me saying, "Don't give them any ideas." Not to worry; they've had these ideas for a long time.

Brodsky and I chatted for a few minutes last week.

Maymin: So, the proposal is basically to move from an opt-in to an opt-out system, where people are presumed to be organ donors unless they explicitly opt out, is that right?

Brodsky: Well, there are many proposals. There is an opt-out proposal. There is also what I call a presumed consent proposal. There are proposals on making it easier to enroll. The fact of the matter is we have a catastrophically fatal system. People are going to die today. The system is not working. People have been dying, in New York, in Connecticut and in America. We can do better. People overwhelmingly want to be organ donors. Sixty-seven percent of people want to be organ donors, but only 11 percent are. Part of that is inertia. Part of that is difficulty in registering. We need to find a system that lets them do that. The choice should be theirs.

What about enforcement against those that disagree? What about people who never made a decision but their family now wants to keep the organs?

I don't know what you are talking about. There is no force here. It is always a choice. These programs have worked in Spain and Israel without any controversy. People can always choose not to donate, and that's fine.

Then why not do it for wealth too? Assume that when people die, all their property, money, house, and everything goes to the state, unless they have explicitly opted out?

That's not anything that's being talked about. And there are no lives at stake there. With organs, there are lives at stake.

But how about allowing those willing to sell their organs to do so?

I would not support that. You are talking about live donations vs. donations done on death.

No, it could be done just on death.

No, I would not support that. We don't do it for blood. We don't do it for anything else. A person's ability to pay should have no effect. There is no virtue to allowing people to traffic in organs. Death traffic is not the way to go. It should not be the case that the wealthy live, while the middle class and poor die.

So what would enforcement of the law look like?

There are no problems. No one is being forced to donate. Each person is making a morally positive choice for themselves.

But if there is no need for enforcement, there is no need for the law.

This program will be accompanied by massive public education. You have to get a driver's license, don't you? That's when you make the choice. Every choice would be an informed choice.

**

Sensing an impasse, we thanked each other and ended the call shortly after. But I wondered: What gives him the right to presume that he can take my organs unless I jump through his hoops?

I know what he would answer. He thinks when lives are at stake, the government can do anything. By that logic, of course, he should, after some reflection, support an opt-out program for a 100-percent estate tax too. If people die without properly filling out the appropriate oval with a #2 pencil, fully and completely, without going outside the oval and without leaving any empty space inside, then their property should go to the state. It could be sold and the proceeds used to alleviate the suffering of the poor, to pay for better medical attention and insurance for those without access to either, to invest in research and development of new drugs and treatments. It could save many lives.

Lives are always at stake. But we are either true humans, true people with truly inalienable rights to life, liberty and property, or we exist at the pleasure of our legislators.

It's fine to disagree with people who have no power over you. But when you are talking to the people who make the laws, you can disagree till you are blue in the face and yellow in the liver, they will still get you, and your organs, in the end.

Originally published on May 13, 2010

LISTEN UP, CHRIS DODD

Research proves all the senator's assumptions about financial regulation are wrong

The Senate passed a 1,500-page financial regulation bill last week after a year of rigorous bipartisan discussions over how, exactly, to get more of your money and put America at greater risk while diverting all blame away from the politicians. Outgoing Connecticut Senator and Banking Committee Chairman Christopher Dodd considered as his personal triumph not just the passage of this bill, but the way it was done — with "full-throated, engaging, vibrant debate on a critical issue in front of our country."

I can attest that Dodd was recently exposed to the most important and relevant information for his bill. I sent him an e-mail a month ago. Here is an abbreviated version, and it included a link to the research mentioned:

"Senator Dodd,

For your banking committee to honestly explore all possible avenues of regulations of risk, you need to be aware of new research findings that I have co-authored. Our research proves, both mathematically and empirically, that ANY regulation of risk will always INCREASE risk, particularly systemic risk. I believe it would be negligent of the committee not to consider the implications of this research because it predicts that specific kinds of regulations that might otherwise be adopted will backfire.

I am available to testify or discuss with you or your staff further at any time."

As you may imagine, Dodd's office called me immediately. They diligently verified every aspect of the proof. They brought in outside experts to check the math and other experts to check the data. When it became clear to everybody that financial regulation of risk will only increase our systemic risk, the chairman himself flew out to see me.

Over the sounds of his helicopter's blades rotating on my front lawn, Dodd thanked me for the research, saying it came just in the nick of time. He called me a national hero. Unbidden, a tear rolled down his cheek as he looked me in the eye and told me his life's goal has been to reduce the risk of financial turmoil, and that up to today, he had always thought that meant we just needed the right rules, the right regulators, the right people in charge. Now he saw that those rules and laws and regulations were actually the cause of the financial collapse. He told me he would abandon the new bill and replace it with a bill to end the Federal Reserve, legalize alternative currencies, shut down the Federal Deposit Insurance Corporation and let any organization that wants to be a bank be a bank, with no further regulation, but saving criminal prosecutions for fraud and theft.

At least, that's what should have happened if this latest addition to the rotting pyramid of regulation truly was the result of a "full-throated, engaging, vibrant debate." Of course, none of it did. My front lawn remains helicopter-free. No one from Dodd's office ever contacted me. Even though I am his constituent. Even though I sent it both to his own account and to that of the committee. Even though the research proves that his bill harms the very goal he claims to espouse.

A pack of wolves deciding just how to storm the chicken co-op is not the definition of a vibrant, engaging debate. Even if the chickens elected those particular wolves instead of others equally vicious. When will chickens stop voting for red and blue wolves?

Originally published on May 27, 2010

HAVE WE LOST THE JIHAD?

Americans are going through a spiritual/philosophical struggle

I was wondering how would we know if we won in Iraq and Afghanistan and couldn't answer the question, so I wondered what it would mean to lose.

There are two forms of jihad. The greater jihad is the internal struggle with one's soul, but the one we are most familiar with is the lesser jihad, the holy war.

The idea of a holy war was first promoted by Islamic military leader Saladin who needed a way to rally his troops to fight to their deaths to retake the lands lost to the Crusades. Jihad was a tool of propaganda, and it worked. Saladin eventually ruled over a vast Middle Eastern empire.

Though much of his original views on jihad were later rejected, the origins seep through to today. Historian and sociologist Maxime Rodinson, writing in 2002, concluded that jihad is still a "propagandistic device which, as need be, resorts to armed struggle."

What is it that today's jihadists are fighting for, if not for land? They are fighting for Islam to rule the world. However, there are many Islamic countries today that differ amongst themselves, so which of their customs and laws does jihad seek to impose?

One way of thinking about it is to ask, what would a unified Islamic government look like? Such a government is called a caliphate, and it was basically the political structure of Islam for hundreds of years, until 1920 when Turkey shucked off the last vestiges of the last caliphate, the Ottoman Empire.

The caliphate was socialist. In a caliphate, the state must own all oil, gas and other fuels; all agricultural land; and all water. Redistribution was a central feature of the caliphate as taxes were collected to pay the poor, the disabled and the elderly. Thus, the caliphate had welfare, universal health insurance and government-funded pensions. The caliphate is widely recognized to have been one of the first welfare states.

The reason for al Qaeda's existence is essentially to establish a caliphate; they make no secret about it — they even call their Internet newscast "The Voice of the Caliphate" — and Osama bin Laden probably wants to be the caliph, the leader of the caliphate.

The caliph is viewed to be virtually perfect and omnipotent, a benevolent dictator in a way. The desire for such firm leadership is not hard to understand — it persists to today in the United States.

Woody Allen has recently lamented that it is too bad that President Obama is not a dictator. "It would be good," Allen said, "if he could be dictator for a few years because he could do a lot of things quickly."

Obama has already done a lot of things quickly. He has effectively nationalized the automobile industry, the banks, the insurance companies and much of America's real estate through the backdoor of mortgage nationalization. He has pushed through universal health insurance. Based on their voting, Americans have seemingly waged an internal struggle for political philosophy, a greater jihad if you will, and concluded that big government is good.

What more is there for jihadists to fight for?

Originally published on June 24, 2010

The Ultimate Currency
Is it time for digital-only dollars?

The nice thing about gold as a currency is that no government can easily and capriciously tax it. Paper money is easy: just print more and spend it however you want. But gold is relatively stable, doesn't go bad, and can be stored easily.

But you can't fit it in your wallet. You can't easily break it into smaller pieces or combine pieces to make larger ones. Gold is not the ultimate currency.

Currency backed by gold is more mobile, but you have to trust someone to exchange your paper or digital claim for actual gold. And if that someone happens to be a government, that trust is guaranteed to be betrayed.

We are living now in an information-driven world. Perhaps currency can be encoded as bits. Even a decade ago, this would have sounded impossible. But because of the widespread dissemination of powerful computing and interconnected networking, some new approaches have recently been developed.

One example is called BitCoin, a free, open-source, peer-to-peer, anonymous, network-based currency. Its creator Satoshi Nakamoto calls it a "cryptocurrency" because there is no way for a middleman to intercept, prevent or tax any exchange of money. Even the users themselves don't necessarily know the real-world identities of who they are dealing with. And there cannot be any inflation or currency manipulation. There is no central database for the police to raid and no way for your bitcoins to be stolen. It's amazing Nakamoto's algorithm is able to guarantee all these benefits.

Imagine it on your iPhone. You walk around and pay for whatever you want without any worries. Even if your phone is stolen, there is no way to access your money without you. It is stable, private, untaxable and uninflatable. Pretty good. It will be great once you can buy groceries with it.

Transactions will always require the BitCoin network. You may think we will always have a network. There's no way the government could interfere with the entire internet, is there? Even China's censorship could probably be twarted by an electronic currency network.

Never underestimate the hunger of a politician. They will always think of a way to use brute force to get your stuff. Our senator Joe Lieberman has proposed a plan that would allow the president to shut down the entire internet for "national security reasons." What could drive a politician to insecurity more than the uneasy feeling that there are some economic transactions happening without his hand in the pie?

The "internet kill switch" has a 120-day limit, after which Congress would rubber-stamp a longer web death. They are all in it together, and when they can't get their coins, you won't get your bits.

They will argue — as they did with the Patriot Act, the invasion of Iraq, the health care bill and all the bailouts — that they are doing this for our own good, to protect us from systemic failure. Wouldn't it be terrible if terrorists could shut down our entire internet? The only way to protect ourselves is to shut it down before they can. Let's shackle ourselves before they do.

The internet itself is virtually unkillable, based on the brilliant way the internet protocol and the transfer control protocol has worked for decades. It automatically reroutes and recovers. It could strike fear into the leeches that polite society calls our elected officials, by circumventing their monopolistic currency in favor of one that actually works.

How about a political kill switch that shuts down Congress for 120 days, unless extended by an anonymous internet poll?

Originally published on July 8, 2010

FINANCIAL SELF-REGULATION
Nothing beats writing your own laws

The Restoring American Financial Stability Act of 2010 is brought to you by the same people who called a curtailment of civil liberties, the Patriot Act, and the imposition of new taxes and substantially no new services for at least half a decade, the Patient Protection and Affordable Care Act. It lives up to Congress' history of misnomers. The act will destabilize the American financial system. It was written by the people it intends to regulate. The same big bankers who got bailed out essentially wrote their own rules going forward. Do you think they wrote those rules to benefit you? (Do you think the health care companies that wrote the health care bill wrote it to benefit you?)

You weren't under the illusion that honorable, vote-fearing politicians wrote every word of every bill, were you? They haven't even read it, let alone written it.

The goal of the regulation seems bold and noble. It claims to protect the American taxpayer by "ending bailouts." But the whole thing is a bailout.

In writing about markets, Adam Smith admitted over two and a half centuries ago that, "People of the same trade seldom meet together, even for merriment and diversion, but the conversation ends in a conspiracy against the public." The difference is that a private cartel can fall apart if even one member defects to take advantage of the artificially high prices. But when the government gets involved, then you are truly conspired against.

There is a simple way to restore American financial stability: get the government out of it. You might ask how to do that, given that it is so entrenched.

Let's run an experiment, a test: let a few new banks opt out of all government regulations. Let them proclaim they are not FDIC-insured nor federally regulated. Let them issue their own currency. Let them make whatever loans they like, and keep as much or as little cash on hand and in reserve that they choose. If they all choose poorly, they will quickly fold because no one will voluntarily give them their hard-earned money. But if they can convince you, personally, to trust them with their money, just as thousands of other companies do when you buy their shares, then why should the both of you be prevented from making an exchange? Why should some politician be able to kill the deal (unless he's getting a kickback for killing it)? Why should the entrenched, big banks be able to prevent this competition?

Andrew Ross Sorkin, author of the bestselling Too Big to Fail, a rich history of what really happened on Wall Street and in Washington over the past few years, interviewed hundreds of the top people involved in the financial crisis. These were all the titans and former titans of bankers, regulators, policymakers and legislators.

I asked him, out of all the people he interviewed, each of whom presumably had an answer for how to prevent this from happening again, how many of them suggested less government, less regulation? How many suggested abolishing the Federal Reserve or federal deposit insurance, or allowing competing currencies, or anything of that nature? His answer was short but telling. "Zero."

The chieftains running the banks today can't even imagine a world where the rules are written by the people and not by the politically connected.

Originally published on July 22, 2010

A CHILLING EFFECT

Your privacy is worthless; Obama's privacy is priceless

Unwinnable wars in Iraq and Afghanistan, enormous expansion of federal health regulations, indefinite detention, targeted killing of American citizens, bungled government responses to environmental disasters, warrantless surveillance and bailouts galore. Are we sure George W. Bush is no longer president?

Barack Obama's administration now wants to be able to see the headers on all e-mails that you send, even if there is no probable cause, no warrant, no judicial oversight and no disclosure to you or anyone else that the FBI even peeked. As far as I can tell, Obama's bill modifying the Electronic Communications Privacy Act would allow the FBI to secretly track information in the from, to, carbon copy and subject fields, among others. The bill would likely also include the history of web sites you visit.

I use terms like "likely" and "as far as I can tell" not only because the language is vague—it would merely insert the four words "electronic communications transactional records" into an ever-growing list of exclusions the FBI can rely on to avoid getting a warrant—but also because there doesn't seem to be any plausible way to object, review, or punish an overbroad or unnecessary FBI investigation.

Meanwhile, just try and find the analogous records between people who communicated with Bush and those who communicated with Obama. Why is it that the two administrations are so similar? Who is pulling the strings? What information could possibly be more important to American security than knowing why two seemingly different individuals continue to pursue the same big-government policies?

Yeah, good luck with that. The law is intended as a one-way peep show only, and we are the ones on a stage with a pole.

One often hears claims that this law or that law will have a "chilling effect" on free speech. The term was part of a 1965 Supreme Court decision striking down an odd postal service law requiring anybody receiving communist political propaganda to specifically authorize receipt before the post office would deliver it. Speech was iced: people could not say what they wanted to say. In a sense, the law was a kind of prior restraint on speech, which is unconstitutional.

How does effectively cc-ing your emails to the FBI and letting them snoop around your browsing history cause a chilling effect? Here's one example. Try to fact check the assertion in the first sentence that Obama continues to approve the "targeted kill" program to authorize an assassination of anybody on earth, including an American citizen like you, at any point in time, even using an unmanned drone, if he decides you are an imminent threat.

Perhaps you might resort to Google, but with what search term? Bear in mind that your search is part of the web address. If you search for "Obama," your address bar will say "q=OBAMA" somewhere in there. That information is likely part of your electronic communications transactional records. Say hi to your local federal agent. How comfortable would you feel searching for the term "Obama target kill?" The FBI may decide to share your name with the Secret Service, under their "better safe than sorry" doctrine.

And when the president also claims the right to assassinate anyone without due process, you may not even have time to regret the loss of your judicial rights if you are deemed an imminent threat.

Originally published on August 5, 2010

MOSQUERADE

In the Lower Manhattan Islamic center debate, everyone is pretending to be something they're not

When it comes to the mosque to be built near Ground Zero in New York City, everyone is pretending to be something they're not.

Perhaps for the first time since Grover Cleveland, a Democratic president is championing private property rights, states' rights and a limited federal government. Barack Obama endorsed the right of Muslims "to build a place of worship and a community center on private property in Lower Manhattan in accordance with local laws and regulation."

Has Obama, of all people, flipped through the Constitution and achieved a clearer understanding of the first, ninth and tenth amendments?

No, it is merely a mask. Otherwise, he would repeal a host of invasive laws. Your First Amendment guarantees to free travel, association, speech and religion are violated whenever your naked body is scanned at an airport, your political book club's reading list is secretly inspected, your phone is tapped without a warrant or your tax dollars are funneled to religious groups and nations that actively fight against your own sacred beliefs. If Obama were sincere, he would end those intrusions and more.

What could or should Obama have said instead? He could have said nothing. It is simply not his place.

This is a rare quality, to be sure. The only politician (other than Ron Paul) who I have ever heard say that something was not his decision was Jesse Ventura, when he was governor of Minnesota. Asked by a reporter about some private entity, though he obviously had a strong personal opinion, Ventura's response was simple and clear. "It is not my call," he essentially said. "It is not within my duties as governor."

Obama could have answered as Ventura did. Instead he chose to inflict his unsolicited opinion on us.

Deep in his heart Obama still denies the intended limited role of the federal government. He thinks it, and he, should be everywhere. He does not fathom that some things are just not his call, whether they be banks, car companies, foreign nations or where LeBron James should have taken his talents.

Most other Democrats actually are silent, refusing to go on the record, probably because they feel, and rightly so, that whatever they say will be used against them. But ironically this silence is a mask for them too. They have donned it not as a principled stand for local autonomy, but purely out of fear for their careers.

Democrats are not alone in their hypocrisy. Republicans who have spent the past decade preaching the need to spread democracy abroad are now upset that democratic institutions at home prevent them from successfully meddling. Republicans have called the project an "unnecessary provocation," an example of "territorial conquest," and "an aggressive act that is clearly offensive." But they don't really think the mosque is a truly violent act. If they did, they would seek to file charges or sue for damages. No, they just want to ride our emotions to get back in power and continue expanding the American empire.

Even Libertarians are hiding behind a mask of tolerance. Citing basic property rights, they argue anybody can build a mosque on any property they own and there is nothing anyone can or should do about it. They are right about the first part, but deeply wrong about the second. There is nothing wrong with voicing disapproval for the mosque. It is an expression of free speech. They may build, but we may protest. True tolerance does not mean you approve of everyone; it means you do not do violence even to those of whom you disapprove.

So far, I too have been hiding behind a mask, the mask of indifference and neutrality, as if I am above these petty issues. But unlike the others, my mask will now come off.

I am deeply offended by the project, for two reasons. First, it strikes me as an ugly ploy. Any religious or political entity that intends to launch on the ten-year anniversary of 9/11 seems disingenuous to me, more interested in its own publicity than in actually doing good.

Second, the name of the entity is nasty. They intend to call it the Cordoba House and the sponsors call themselves the Cordoba Initiative, both named after the city in Spain where, they say, Jews, Christians, and Muslims co-existed peacefully. Theirs is the most contemptible mask of all, because what they don't say is how that peace ended. Fundamentalist Muslims gave all its residents a choice: convert to Islam or die. My great-great-great-…-grandfather Maimonides took his family and fled. In my mind, the name Cordoba does not conjure images of peace and co-existence.

By their logic, they would see nothing wrong with opening a German cultural center in downtown Tel Aviv called the Dachau House. After all, there was a time when Jews and Gentiles lived peaceably side-by-side in that pleasant Munich suburb.

Originally published on August 19, 2010

MISSION ACCOMPLISHED AGAIN
Military operations in Iraq still aren't actually over

By the time you read this, President Barack Obama will have addressed the nation about Iraq. How will he have phrased the fact that we still have 50,000 troops stationed in a country that has never posed an actual threat to our national sovereignty?

Unfortunately the terms "end of major combat operations" and "mission accomplished" were already taken, back when we first "won" in 2003. It looks like the euphemism du jour will be "the final departure of combat troops." We're perilously close to running out of ways to proclaim victory while continuing to fight.

Our remaining troops are supposedly there just to provide training, logistical support, encouragement and a kind smile. We are but as friendly advisers.

That's a charade.

About a decade ago, I was a trader at a hedge fund that had opened a branch in Tokyo. Due to convoluted regulations, we had not yet been granted all of the operating licenses for trading. So any time we wanted to do a trade, we had to do a three-way conference call with the Japanese broker and our own branch back in Greenwich. We would then say to our Greenwich counterpart, "I advise you to do this trade," and describe the trade. The poor sleepy person whose turn it was to babysit us on the night shift would stifle a yawn and say, "Okay, I would like to do that," at which point the infinitely patient Japanese broker would confirm that the trade was actually done.

It was delightfully stupid. We all knew the trade was effectively done long before the formal approval. It was all a charade, a farce of government bureaucracy. It was also temporary. Once the requirements were filled, we dispensed with the formality.

But in Iraq, we are just now introducing the formality. Our remaining troops will "advise" the locals just as we in Tokyo "advised" Greenwich. The Iraqi soldiers, just like the Japanese brokers, have no illusions about who is calling the shots. If there was ever a problem with a trade, the advisers were always the people on the hook, not the formal acknowledgers. And if there is ever an issue with the insurgency, everybody knows who is still calling the shots.

One of Osama bin Laden's primary grievances was the presence of American troops in Saudi Arabia. In 2003, we withdrew all of our troops from there. Now, Iraqis, who are understandably upset about a continuing military presence in their country, have both an easy recruitment pitch and a roadmap to success. They can just point across their southern border and say, "See? We can get the troops to leave here too. Terrorism works."

Everybody, starting with Obama, is going to try to put their own spin on the fact that 50,000 troops remain in Iraq, and they will do it by framing, a psychological technique to change your perspective. Democrats will frame it relative to campaign promises and say there are fewer troops there now than there have been in years. Republicans will frame it relative to past military activity and say that the only reason we can have fewer troops now is because we had more troops back then.

Both of those are just spin. At the heart of the matter, we still have thousands of troops in a foreign land. The correct frame is relative to zero. Do we still have more than zero troops in Iraq?

Originally published on September 1, 2010

The Government Can't "Create" Jobs
Jobs come about as naturally as species do

President Barack Obama announced this week the largest arms deal in American history, selling $60 billion of military equipment to Saudi Arabia. Apparently a primary consideration in this deal was that an estimated 75,000 jobs would be created.

Job creation seems to be a common goal for both government parties. Politicians seem to all be job creationists. Biological creationists believe a single creator made all the variety of life we see today. Job creationists believe a single entity created all the variety of jobs we see today.

Biological creationists ignore fossil evidence showing evolution across time. They claim that the seemingly sudden changes in observed species are proof of a creator rather than evidence of fitness winning out. Job creationists ignore historical evidence showing that freedom increases wealth across time. They claim that the seemingly sudden shifts in types of jobs from agricultural to industrial to service-oriented are proof of a government-controlled economy rather than evidence of an elastic labor market.

Biological creationists ignore experimental science, even though anybody can easily select desired features for fruit flies and have an adapted and evolved generation within a few days. Job creationists ignore competition showing wealth creation, even though anyone can hire a group of people and have a trained and capable workforce within a few days.

Biological creationists ignore DNA and focus on the animals themselves. They make up words like "micro-evolution" and distinguish them from "macro-evolution" by claiming that a tornado in a junkyard wouldn't create a jet plane. Job creationists ignore people and focus on the job titles themselves. They make up words like "micro-economics" and distinguish them from "macro-economics" by claiming that a mob on a rampage wouldn't build office towers and factories.

But the facts are indisputable. Your pet dog and your television set, respectively, are proof that each kind of creationist is just plain wrong. Evolution and freedom produced both.

On a recent episode of "The Simpsons," Lisa marvels at a beautiful fish Ned Flanders displays. "Mr. Flanders," she asks, "how did you make these amazing fish?"

"Actually, God made some fish that were pretty close to these," Ned replies, "so naturally we selected those for further breeding."

Lisa might well have asked Obama how he made so many jobs. The free market had already created all sorts of specialized jobs, from welder to designer to blueprint ink maker, and Obama just paid more to those who did the jobs he wanted to spread.

Lisa then asks, "So that natural selection was the origin of this species?"

"Yep, that's exactly — ," Ned starts, and then laughs. "You almost got me."

One of Ned's fishes then grows some legs, crawls out of the water, and starts breathing air. "Not on my watch!" he says, and pushes it back into the water.

And that's exactly what job creationists are doing with our economy. How many free jobs have been drowned to legitimize the job creationists' false beliefs?

Originally published on September 16, 2010

GLENN BECK THE SOCIALIST
Libertarian or phony usurper?

Glenn Beck is a polarizing person among libertarians. Some laud him for being one of the few voices on television to criticize both Democrats and Republicans as being equally complicit in growing the size of government and pointing out that there is no significant difference between them. Others view him as a phony usurper of the freedom movement.

This raises even more interesting questions than just about Beck himself: what makes a person a phony? At what point can a person with formerly statist views be considered to have had an authentic change of heart?

The funny thing is that those who think he is a true libertarian tend to watch him; those that think he is a fake do not. I was one of those who did not, and it caused a lot of debate with those who did. Why not watch him? He is interesting, he raises good questions, and so on.

I finally watched him last night as he discussed the book *Nudge* by Richard Thaler and Cass Sunstein. Thaler was my dissertation advisor a few years ago when I received my Ph.D. in Finance from the University of Chicago. I read an early version of their book. I even provided an extra Simpsons reference for them. I am mentioned in the acknowledgments. I have read every single post on the *Nudge* blog, sent them useful links, and commented on items. In short, I am intimately familiar with the themes and the content of *Nudge*.

Watching Beck, I discovered the truth about him: neither those who claim him as a libertarian nor those that denounce him as a phony are right. Beck is not a libertarian; he is a deep-seated socialist. But he is also not a phony; it is so deep-seated in him that he doesn't even realize it.I had three problems with Beck's show. The first is that he provides the right conclusions but he gets there with the wrong arguments. This is extraordinarily frustrating to watch. Suppose you like a girl, or a boy. Or you find a particular religious text magnificent. Then imagine how you would feel hearing someone praise your girl or boy, or your religious text, but for all the wrong reasons. You want to simultaneously object and agree. Yes, the object of your heart is wonderful, but not at all in that way. "Thumbelina is beautiful. She is so tall!" Huh?

Beck's main message is that if governments nudge people to do the right thing by changing their default options, then that will eventually lead to riots and the collapse of society. I do agree that government nudges are a bad idea. But Beck's argument is essentially a slippery slope argument. And there are two big problems with slippery slope arguments.

First, regardless of disclaimers to the contrary, they implicitly assume that the current proposal in and of itself is harmless — for example, replacing the default choice of unhealthy fries with healthier carrots in, say, a kid's meal. That's giving up on the fight. Perhaps there is some truth to the slippery slope, that indeed in a world where we accept government regulations of defaults we will become more acquiescent of further government interventions. But that will never win you any converts. "We'll just deal with it later," people will think. Or they will suggest we just vote on the current proposal and when the really bad stuff comes, we can revisit it then. A slippery slope is a vacuous coun-terargument because it leaves the person you are trying to sway simply feeling that this current proposal, whatever it is, is not so bad by itself.

Second, a slippery slope argument does not bind the person arguing. In other words, Beck leaves himself wiggle room to lat-er change his mind completely and support nudge-like policies. How? He can just say, "A-ha! I have discovered a way to block the slippery slope. We just need to also do X, and that's it." Then with some magic, the fries lead not to riots, but to world peace. There is no intellectual commitment with a slippery slope argument. My second problem with Beck was his exaggerations and misstatements of major issues. If all I had known of *Nudge* had been from watching his show, and then I was to debate Thaler or Sunstein, they would destroy me. Numerous times Beck claimed that nudges remove or restrict options. Thaler would quite clearly argue that this is not so, and he would win that argument hands down. Most nudge policies are simply about changing defaults, such as the default 401k plan you in-vest in, or the default health plan you choose. You can always choose whatever you would have otherwise chosen, if you so wish. But those who don't care or don't know would be opted into a better plan, not as viewed by Thaler or even Beck, but as viewed by people just like them, or in some cases, even by themselves.

There are ways to argue against nudging people through government force. But slippery slopes and false statements are not good ones.

How would I argue against *Nudge*? First, I would point out that it is wonderful and completely unarguable when it comes to private companies or households. It probably is a great idea to hide the fatty foods in your kitchen and make the healthier ones more easily available. You will probably snack a little better. If you run a company providing pensions to your employees, why not default them into what you and other employees clearly view to be the best alternative, rather than just bonds or just stocks? Whoever disagrees can easily change it, but whoever didn't think about it wouldn't regret it much later. Perhaps you disagree with an example here or there, but at heart *Nudge* provides a set of useful tools to help people without being abrasive. In a private, free market setting, that is hard to argue against. It is hard not to cheer for it.

Second, I would point out that when it comes to government nudges, it is not the same thing. Government nudges are wrong. I have had this debate with Thaler and we disagree. He thinks libertarians are irrelevant because we don't address practical questions. I think governments that implement nudges in areas they are not supposed to intervene are continuing their unconstitutional activities. Should the default military armor for soldiers who can choose otherwise be X or Y when we are fighting an unconstitutional war of aggression? I don't think it is being irrelevant to say that that question is silly, and that the bigger question of non-interventionism ought to be addressed.

But Beck does not make a single case against immoral government behavior. In fact, he agrees with the principle. And this is the third, and biggest, problem that I have with him.

He started and ended his show with the same scenario, saying that America is facing a choice, a choice between socialism and freedom. And that while there are some that support socialism, there are more of us who support freedom, and books like *Nudge* are implicitly supporting socialism without actually saying so, and therefore depriving the American people of the debate. Let's just have it out in the open, he says, and let the people decide.

And that's where he is most wrong. Some things are absolutely not up to the people to decide. If a majority voted to execute an innocent person without due process, that is wrong. If they voted for genocide, that is wrong. Morality and majority vote are not the same thing.

But Beck thinks they are. And that's where he reveals his statism and his socialism. Majority vote is the very basis of socialism. But true libertarians know that even 95 percent of a county can be wrong. And the important fight is to win the war in the hearts and minds of people with truth and actual engagement of the details, not sweeping things under the rug, arguing about slippery slopes, or playing clips of a handful of people.

Beck does not realize he is a socialist. It is an unstated assumption of his that of course we should leave it up to the people.

We've tried that, Glenn. When people can vote themselves your property, they will.

The fundamental tenet of socialism is that whatever the people say is right.

The fundamental tenet of libertarianism is that the initiation of force is wrong.

By explicitly and continually arguing that we need to all make a decision together, Beck has shown himself to be a socialist at heart. It is almost as if he is saying, "Look, I would prefer freedom, but if the people vote for socialism, then that's okay."

Glenn, it is not okay.

Originally published on September 16, 2010

EINSTEIN WAS WRONG WHEN IT CAME TO SOCIALISM

Socialism caused the famed physicist to reject all the foundations of science

Albert Einstein was one of the smartest scientists ever. But when it came time for him to convince others of his socialist views, he essentially rejected all of the foundations of science.

Science is founded on facts, models and experiments. Facts are basic observations about reality anybody can confirm. Models are the stories that we tell to explain the world in a useful way. Logic lets us develop the new predictions of our models, and experiments let us test them.

A few years before his death, in the inaugural article for an American socialist magazine, Einstein argued that the facts we have observed about economics have emerged from at least somewhat capitalistic systems and therefore must all be discarded in discussions of how to overcome such "predatory" systems.

He also claimed that models for economics are difficult because "observed economic phenomena are often affected by many factors which are very hard to evaluate separately." Furthermore, the models of economics we have learned have been foisted on us by immoral "conquering peoples" who have controlled our education; therefore we must dispose of all models that are not socialistic.

Even logic fell by the wayside after socialism invaded Einstein's soul. "Science cannot create ends," he explained. "Science, at most, can supply the means." So who can supply the ends? "The ends themselves are conceived by personalities with lofty ethical ideals." Einstein left unstated who these lofty personalities are who ought to control our lives.

Einstein abandoned all of the foundations of knowledge and truth. He wrote, quite plainly, "We should be on our guard not to overestimate science and scientific methods when it is a question of human problems."

"Man can find meaning in life," he asserted, "only through devoting himself to society."

He was totally and utterly wrong. You and I have found meaning in our lives without devoting ourselves to society. It's not a model, because it doesn't explain the world. It's certainly not logical. In fact it's self-contradictory. To devote to a cause means to willingly give yourself over to it. But if every individual gives himself over to a society, then there is no longer any will left to oversee and manage the devotion. And it would fail by experiment. You and I are counterexamples.

Einstein envisioned a centrally planned economy, a single world government, with all means of production publicly owned, with work distributed equally among all those who are able, with a guaranteed livelihood to every person on Earth, and with an educational system oriented towards social goals.

What would Einstein do with those who were able to work but didn't want to? Or those who wanted to exchange some of their guaranteed livelihood today for a chance at great wealth tomorrow (and were willing to risk poverty for it)? Or those daydreamers who wanted to challenge accepted principles? Would he simply educate all the ambition out of them?

Socialism is a worm, a worm that even Einstein couldn't shake. If the greatest physicist of the twentieth century can succumb to the socialist infestation, then anybody can. Perhaps our only defense is to maintain an even stricter adherence to the search for truth than he did. When it came to politics, Einstein was no Einstein.

Originally published on September 30, 2010

THE PRIVACY GAP

Politicians do care about privacy—their own

Imagine a world without any privacy whatsoever. Some military nanotechnology gone wrong releases trillions of tiny particle-sized recorders and rebroadcasters. These little guys are so small they can penetrate walls and clothing and are invisible even up to enormous magnification. And all they do is record a little snippet of all the wavelengths in their immediate vicinity — audio, video, infrared, ultraviolet, etc.— and rebroadcast them. The rebroadcasts get bounced around just like the chunks of data that send email all over the world. There is no way to shut them down or stop them. Perhaps they even spawn new versions of themselves.

Each little bit of recorded data is geotagged and timed and within seconds will circumnavigate the globe. If you just eavesdrop on the rebroadcasts and assemble together those chunks that are nearby in time and space to your point of interest, you can piece together an entire scene, from every possible angle. Someone will develop software where all you need to enter is a latitude, longitude and time to see and hear what happened there and then, from angles and changes in viewpoint that automatically mimic how a director would edit the scene together.

There is no way to hide. You can shut the curtains, hide under a blanket and only use hand signals, but it would not be hard to reinterpret the infrared radiation into a more clearly visible picture. You can't use a vacuum to suck out all the little bugs any more than you can suck out all the electrons and neu-trinos from a portion of space.

Crimes would be much easier to solve. Who did it? He did. Right there, see? With just a modicum of facial recognition technology, a reality search engine could find where your kids or spouse or favorite athlete is at any moment. Professional sports would be played in empty gymnasiums with players wearing ad-vertisements on their jersey since that is their only remaining source of revenue; who would pay to attend or watch on TV what they can see for free and from any angle?

Our generation would be upset, but eventually people would get used to it. Everybody poops; get over it. And what could we do? The little guys are too small and too numerous to catch or destroy. The next generation would grow up knowing that they could rewind to any moment in history, from their births on, and see and hear exactly what happened, from any angle. Cell phones came and changed the world, then the inter-net, now this. We always adapt. Eventually.

But what about politicians? What about the government? They would also notice that they can't do anything about the recorders and rebroadcasters. But they could do something about the viewers. They could pass laws against viewing certain times or places. They could pass laws about using or developing or aiding in the distribution of particular software. They could viciously prosecute anyone who violated their privacy. It is in the interests of national security, they will claim.

But even if they can keep Americans from seeing the truth, they can't prosecute the whole world, unless all of the politicians join together to make one world government with a strong centralized police force. In other words, global tyranny. All to keep the politicians in power.

Politicians don't care about privacy overall. They care only about the difference in privacy between them and us. When they pass laws to make spying on us easier for them, arguments about violating our privacy mean nothing to them. They simply don't understand the problem.

But when you try to find some transparency about government — who exactly has the Fed given money to, who really drafted the health care bill, what machinations are being used on government statistics and reporting, exactly how much gold is left in Fort Knox, etc. — the answer invariably comes back: none of your business.

Perhaps from our perspective we too ought not to care so much about the overall level of privacy. That is something that technology can and does transform over time. Perhaps we also ought to care about the differential privacy between us and them. At least a little.

Originally published on October 14, 2010

DEATH AND TAXES

How the government will calculate the cost of a human life

If you are old and wealthy and want to pass as much on to your kids as you can, you better kick the bucket this year. If you pass away after Dec. 31, the government will seize more than half of your estate as the temporary death tax exemption expires.

This enormous incentive could cause people to die earlier in ways as direct and conscious as a planned suicide or as subtle and subconscious as a skipped medication. How many people? We don't know. But tax laws are designed to change people's behaviors and at least some people respond to some incentives some of the time. So, some people will die earlier than they otherwise would, solely because of taxes.

Congress communicates to the citizens how it wants them to behave by punishing what it doesn't like and rewarding, or at least refraining from punishing, what it does. Congress decided it wants people to buy houses with debt; that's why you can deduct interest but not principal on your taxes. This year, dying is being rewarded. Next year, dying will be punished.

Anyone with an estate who decides to die this year is not being anymore unethical, or anymore heroic, than a new homeowner with a big debt. They are just individuals trying to do what is best for themselves and their families, given the laws imposed on them.

In the future, as health care becomes more and more of a government service, there may come a time when the cost of keeping someone alive will exceed the amount that individual would be willing to die to pass on. There wouldn't be any direct bartering between a bureaucrat and the patient, but the laws may change once more. There may be another zero-death-tax year to encourage people to die.

And that may not be enough. We may need to consider death subsidies, in which the government taxes some people to pay others to die. For those whose health care costs become astronomically high, wouldn't it make sense to give their heirs an extra million instead of keeping them alive, in pain and discomfort, for the same price? Or make it a thousand bucks to your heirs if you agree to a cheap but risky surgery instead of life support. It doesn't have to be guaranteed death; it could just be a higher probability. Not to worry! Congress will work out the details.

If you are recoiling at these suggestions, I am with you. It is disgusting. But many other laws share the same flaw. If a death subsidy is appalling, then so is a paid military engaged in a war of aggression. We are taxed to pay others to die. FDA restrictions on medical treatment leave sick people fewer options. The war on drugs makes people go to shady neighborhoods instead of corner drug stores. We are taxed to support institutions that force people who just want to live their own lives and to take on more lethal risks. Again, we are taxed to pay others to die.

Every time a law keeps you from peaceably doing what you would have preferred, you are relegated to choosing among second-best alternatives — perhaps riskier alternatives. Just about every action of government involves taxing some people to restrict others. Those others now face more risk. Some will die.

Surely, government must pass laws against non-peaceful acts, and it may tax to enforce those laws; that is the legitimate purpose of government. But that accounts for a tiny fraction of current government spending. Every other item is just a death subsidy in disguise.

Originally published on November 11, 2011

UNCLE SAM RESPONDS TO WARREN BUFFET

Billionaire investor Warren Buffett wrote a "thank you" note to "Uncle Sam" in the Nov. 16 issue of The New York Times, sincerely defending the $700 billion "bailout" of the economy passed in September 2008. This is a response.

My dearest nephew Warren,

Thank you for your kind note. I especially appreciate your delivery method. Most people use my postal service to send me mail, but that never works. My employees just throw all that stuff in with the letters to Santa.

I like that you put your letter to me in The New York Times. It is one of my favorites. I am even thinking of nationalizing it if need be. After all, we can't sully quality journalism with such crass concerns as profit. And who better to maintain standards of truth and accuracy than me?

Very few people understand me as well as you do, Warren. You have a gift. Most people think I caused the financial crisis with too many regulations and too much meddling in the economy. But it takes a genius of your caliber to understand that it was really the result of a "mass delusion," as you put it.

The crisis was that the people were "losing trust by the hour in institutions they once revered." I couldn't have put it better myself. The people were wrong, not the government. Not me. Never me. I once thought I was wrong, but then I thought better of it. There is no room for doubt at the top, Warren. We are in a constant state of emergency, and we have been for about a century now.

One of my proudest accomplishments has been to take the fight out of the Americans. "I want you!" That's my favorite phrase. The people used to be so cynical, so wary of government. Where was the love? Where was, as you put it, the reverence? Fortunately, with massive spending, endless war, centralized banking and public education, I have been able to mold them into proper people, people who have respect for authority.

Warren, you so deeply understand the benefits of centralized power that I will have my current puppet Barack Obama give you a Presidential Medal of Freedom. Because what is freedom ultimately but the ability of the government to do what is best for its flock?

I am especially pleased, Warren, that you noticed that during the time of emergency, I was able to "stretch legal boundaries" and disregard "slowdowns, like Congressional hearings and studies." You also astutely noticed that my financial henchmen, like Ben Bernanke, Hank Paulson and Tim Geithner, are my "troops." It is a war out there, Warren.

There are still some untamed Americans. Do you know how to tame a wild elephant? You tie it up to a thick metal post when it is young. You beat it savagely but talk to it in a soothing voice so that it learns you are the master. You make it afraid, hungry, thirsty and hurt, until it stops resisting. It takes about a week to break them. After that, they are yours. You can then tie them with a thin string to a wooden post, and even train them to pick up the wooden post when it is time to move. They could just walk away, but they stop trying to escape. They are trained.

But Americans are a much more stubborn bunch. It's been 100 years and some of them are still not broken. They object to basic security checks at airports. They claim things like privacy. Since when do sheep have privacy!

We still have work to do, Warren. There are still some Americans in America.

Your uncle always,
Sam

Originally published on November 19, 2010

END DIPLOMACY

Bargaining with other nations is another messy, unnecessary, power-grabbing habit of the state

The recent leaking of correspondence between the U.S. Department of State and its missions abroad shows that we seem to treat our diplomats as spies, encouraging them to root around and report the secrets they find. One can imagine other countries do the same or even more; diplomacy and espionage have gone hand-in-hand for centuries.

Henry Kissinger defined diplomacy in many ways but perhaps most usefully as "the art of relating states to each other by agreement rather than by the exercise of force." Sounds reasonable, right?

It is reasonable, if you replace "states" with "corporations." A corporation is an entity with a specific mandate and governance. It is more than reasonable for an officer of a corporation to negotiate with other corporations; it could be that person's entire job. And no employee could justifiably complain about any negotiation taking part, even if it would substantially alter that employee's job, because the employee is being paid for his or her time. About the only way the employee could dissent would be as a loyal objector, arguing the negotiated policy is bad for the company as a whole.

But the sole legitimate function of states is to enforce the rights of their citizens. To the extent the state controls or regulates production, it is a mixture of both a corporation and a state, but with two key differences: "employees" of corporate states do not get paid, and they can never quit.

A standard textbook, *Diplomacy: Theory and Practice*, defines diplomacy as "communications between officials designed to promote foreign policy either by formal agreement or tacit adjustment." This just means diplomacy is a tool of foreign policy and the foreign policy itself is the question.

The best foreign policy, and the one with the longest history in America, is non-interventionism. Thomas Paine's Common Sense argued against alliances with other countries. George Washington beseeched us in his farewell address to "have as little political connection as possible" with other countries. Thomas Jefferson famously summarized the policy as "peace, commerce, and honest friendship with all nations, entangling alliances with none." Non-interventionism just means keeping our political heads down. It is different from isolationism, which seeks to avoid trade among nations. On the contrary, non-interventionism allows anybody to trade with anybody else, but they have to negotiate the deals themselves.

A recent book on foreign service as a career, *Career Diplomacy: Life and Work in the U.S. Foreign Service*, takes seriously the question of why we need diplomacy at all. The authors list its primary mission as advancing our "national interests" abroad.

Is it at least possible that a country of several million people has conflicting interests? Domestically, we are able to negotiate amongst ourselves. Why not let us negotiate with others as well? Other nations also have millions of citizens with conflicting interests. Let the benefiting parties each find themselves. People are quite capable of advancing their own interests.

If America followed the policy of non-interventionism, we would see a massive reduction in all branches of the military, including the foreign service. We would bring home just about all of our troops and diplomats. We'd have more prosperity and more freedom as a result of the increased trade and the decreased terrorism.

The newly leaked documents tell us what we knew all along: Diplomats advance not the many and varied interests of the people, but the single, overarching interest of the state to usurp as much power as possible for itself.

Originally published on December 8, 2010

BINGE SPENDING
How to trim the tummy of big government

In 1978, researcher Thomas J. Coates published a cute, three-page case study on a 30-year-old college senior. Now, this is before our time, and perhaps college seniors were older back then, or perhaps this was just one particular guy. I don't know. But this guy had been overweight, by 15 to 40 percent, for his entire life. Three years prior to Coates' study, he had started to straighten up. He went from 225 pounds to 145 and was then 10-percent underweight.

At the time of the research, the guy was taking finals and stressing out. (Perhaps he was worried about next year being a 31-year-old college senior.) He would often wake up and drink some water or diet soda from the fridge.

"One night," the paper ominously observes, "he noticed some pastry in the refrigerator and ate it."

Cue the dramatic music. We all know what happened from here. It unleashed an appetite he never knew he had. Three weeks after that first pastry, he had eaten, in one night, one-and-a-half apples, a bowl of Jell-O, a pint of ice cream, three plums, a chicken thigh, a slice of bread, two nectarines, half a pound of fish, three crackers, 1.5 cups of plain yogurt and an English muffin. Adding together the nutritional values of each of these using the computational knowledge engine WolframAlpha.com, they amount to 2,827 calories, more than his total daily requirement.

Until World War I, America had followed a foreign policy of non-interventionism. Government spending as a percentage of gross domestic product never exceeded ten percent. Then we declared war on Germany. We ate our first pastry.

Our government didn't run amok immediately. Within a few years, government spending had stabilized back to about ten percent of our overall production, but always just a little above. We never dipped below ten percent again.

Then came the 1930s and government spending ratcheted up to 20 percent. Then World War II kicked it up to near 50 for a few years before stabilizing at around 30 percent, which is roughly where it stayed until the last few years. Now we've permanently established camp on the 40 percent plateau.

Of course, there is a major difference between the binge eater and the binge politician — the eater wanted to stop. He wanted to control himself.

The first thing he did was place stickers on the fridge saying, "STOP! THINK!" This did not work. He was too sleepy to even notice them. Next he began placing furniture in the hall to wake himself up enough to think about what he was doing. Still no luck.

Undeterred, he tried paying his friends cash, to be repaid only if he didn't eat. It became more expensive to binge, but binge he still did.

He tried tying up his refrigerator with twine before going to sleep, but with knives in the kitchen, he just cut the cord. So then he tried also hiding all his knives in the trunk of his car in the garage. This was a mixed success.

The government is not some external force imposed on us. We vote for these people. But polls widely show Americans preferring smaller government and less spending. So how do we control ourselves from voting for the candidate who offers us a bigger pastry at the expense of our neighbors?

You could wear buttons and stickers supporting your favorite candidate. Here's a good slogan: "STOP! THINK!" It won't work here either.

You could make it physically difficult for yourself to vote or support any candidate, recognizing that they're all the same anyway. But somebody will end up voting, even if it is just the candidates and their mothers.

You could make politicians and candidates promise to spend less, or even enforce a balanced budget amendment, or any other limitations. But that's just twine on a fridge. You would constantly feel anxious because you know whichever lobbyist reaches those knives first will get the lion's share of the earmarks and pork.

The only thing that can work for government is the only thing that worked for the binge eater, who ultimately stumbled onto a simple solution: refrigerator locks. He would lock the fridge every night. When he awoke, the chains and locks couldn't be broken in to, but he was also not anxious anymore.

If government is locked up and simply cannot take from one to give to another, a lot of our nation's anxieties would disappear.

Let's hope it's not too late to put Uncle Sam on a diet.

Originally published on December 21, 2010

LABOR, MATH, AND LOVE

What does it cost to be left alone?

The federal government has 2 million employees. Across all states, there are 4 million more state government employees and 11 million more local government employees. (Connecticut has 57,117 state government employees and 108,972 local government employees.) That means there is a grand total of 17 million people whose wages are paid by our taxes.

In the meantime, unemployment is now a big problem, largely yet ironically due to the regulations, laws, and management of these 17 million people in grinding our economy to a halt. There are about 9 million people collecting unemployment checks right now, with about half of those from temporary emergency measures and half on more conventional unemployment. There are another 6 million or so who are unemployed but not receiving any money from the government.

In other words, unemployment is a huge problem because there are about 15 million jobless. But there are even more government employees in America than there are unemployed people. If we simply cut 15 million of the 17 million government jobs in America and returned the taxes to the people who earned the money, we could see how many of those laid off would be rehired at the same wages in a free market.

What if we really did cut government spending at all levels by 90 percent, eliminated 90 percent of all regulations, and reduced the government workforce by 90 percent? Would we be facing double the unemployment numbers from all of the laid-off government workers? Would children go hungry? Would the world end?

Or would letting people keep what they earn mean they could spend more of it on the ones they love? Would it simply mean that unconstitutional wars remained unfought, that our privacy remained uninvaded, that our traveling personal parts remained ungroped and unphotographed, and that politically favored companies remained unbailed-out?

Slashing spending means we can slash both taxes and our debt. When someone offers you a job, you don't have to consider your silent partner's cut. Just about all of it would go into your pocket. That means the economy can skyrocket again, once it shuffles off these government foils that trade is heir to. Virtually all of the unemployed, including former government employees, would be able to find better, more rewarding jobs.

The transition back to a free America doesn't have to hurt anybody. Income redistribution programs could be phased out over a period of a few years, on a strict schedule. Or they could even be wiped out overnight in exchange for a fixed lump sum payment. Would you agree to never receive any Social Security, Medicare, Medicaid, ObamaCare, public education, unemployment insurance, etc., for a one-time payment of $100,000 and guaranteed tax-free status for all income you or your children or their children ever earned? Even if every American household jumps at that proposal, that would still cost far less than running our government in the same bloated way we have been for the past few years. It's a win-win!

Beyond the economic arguments for drastically reducing the size of our government at all levels, there is also the emotional argument. There is such a thing as love. And love means you care about some people more than you care about others. You love particular people; others love others. We don't all love everybody in the same way. So what is the justification in using violence to force others to support those they love less at the expense of those they love more?

Some people would have you believe that we need government for a social safety net, to help those who fall through the cracks, or to offset individual selfishness with bureaucratic indifference. They don't acknowledge the fact that forced income redistribution is forced love redistribution. Instead, they say it only hurts a few people and it only hurts them a little bit and they can afford it and they were asking for it anyway and they may even enjoy it. These are disgusting sentiments.

Love cannot be forced. And yet we currently employ millions to do just that.

Maybe it's time our government pillaged us less and respected us more.

Originally published on January 4, 2011

LOWER THE DEBT CEILING

Let the politicians suffer the consequences of ruining America's credit rating

The big faux debate in Washington these days is whether or not the federal debt limit should be raised. Congress needs to pass a new law each time the government reaches its previous limit on how much money it can borrow. Over the past 70 years, they have raised it more than once a year on average.

In other words, the debt limit is not a limit at all. It's just a formality. It's as if you set yourself a goal to have a balance of less than $3,000 on your credit card bills. Then, after reaching $3,000, you adjust your goal to $3,500, then $4,000, and so on. You will eventually reach the credit card's externally imposed limit. But what's the external limit on America's debt capacity?

The government currently owes about $14 trillion. Could they borrow $100 trillion? That's approximately the total amount of wealth on earth. If everybody sold everything they owned at current market value and paid off all their own debts, they would have about $100 trillion or so that they could then lend to the federal government of America. But if everybody sold everything, who would buy it? The only entity with cash: the federal government. In other words, all of humanity would end up with no property except IOUs from a consortium of politicians. Maybe that's what they have in mind.

The debt limit game is not confined to either of the two major government parties. Democrats and Republicans alike vote to raise the limit, raise spending, raise taxes, raise troops and raze countries. This year, Republicans are making a big deal over the debt ceiling. But it is a fake argument and not a principled stand — the same way Congress initially voted against the $700 billion Wall Street bailout. Politicians simply try to get the most they can for whoever funds them. Congress quickly voted for the bailout when a myriad of pork projects magically appeared in a revised version. And the Republicans will vote in favor of increasing the debt limit once their lobbyists get paid.

But for us ordinary Americans, the debt limit is our friend. Although the friction it provides against more rampant government spending is modest at best, it is still more resistance than we provide through words or actions or petitions.

Suppose we all write letters to our elected representatives, flooding them with calls to not only refuse to increase the debt limit, but to actually lower it. Following the will of the people would leave the politicians without any money to redistribute to their friends. They would reply with solemn form letters about how they agreed with our values and ideals and would also like to see a smaller, more efficient government, but at this time of emergency, "we" need to raise the debt limit, temporarily, and thank you for your continued support.

Who is "we"? It is not you and me. It is them, the politicians.

Perhaps we, meaning the true, you-and-me we, should insist not just on a lower debt limit, but on a debt limit of zero dollars. It is not we the people who owe $14 trillion. It is the federal government. It is a bunch of empty suits, politicians long since retired or passed away or merely lacking ethics, who have burdened our country. If creditors want their money back, they should talk to those suits. They can't come after your car or your house. Let the politicians pay off their debt.

And if they can't, then let them default, and let the creditors come after the assets of the politicians, not the assets of the innocent citizens. Those who argue against a default cry that one of the dangerous results would be a far lower credit rating for the future debt of America. But that's good! Let's hope someday the credit rating of America is so junky, because the government is no longer able to seize or steal the assets of its citizens, that no one would ever loan the federal government money. Then they would have nobody to borrow from. And the debt ceiling would be at zero, right where it belongs.

Originally published on February 2, 2011

DILBERT AND THE U.S. BUDGET
A discussion with Dilbert creator Scott Adams

Though I have never met him, Dilbert creator Scott Adams is one of my favorite people. His comics have brought me joy for many years. I take his books on vacations, especially on beaches, where other people often ask to borrow them. He is the author of numerous books and also what is possibly the most widely read ebook in the world, God's Debris. His incredibly successful comic strip "Dilbert" needs no introduction. On his blog, he has covered a wide variety of topics. Most recently, he asked for a volunteer to discuss how to cut the U.S. budget without increasing taxes. The below is reproduced verbatim from Scott's blog at dilbert.com/blog with his kind permission. –PM

In a recent post I asked for a worthy volunteer to be interviewed on the topic of balancing the U.S. budget by expense cuts alone, without making things worse. (Full disclosure: I believe this to be impossible.) The most qualified volunteer, and the person with the most votes from readers of this blog, is Phil Maymin.

Borrowing from the bio on Phil's website at http://philmaymin.com/about-phil...

Dr. Phil Maymin is Assistant Professor of Finance and Risk Engineering at NYU-Polytechnic Institute. He is also the founding managing editor of Algorithmic Finance.

He holds a Ph.D. in Finance from the University of Chicago, a Master's in Applied Mathematics from Harvard University, and a Bachelor's in Computer Science from Harvard University. He also holds a J.D. from Northwestern California University School of Law and is an attorney at law admitted to practice in California.

He has been a portfolio manager at Long-Term Capital Management, Ellington Management Group, and his own hedge fund, Maymin Capital Management.

He is also an award-winning journalist, a policy scholar for a free market think tank, a Justice of the Peace, a former Congressional candidate, a columnist for the *Fairfield County Weekly* and *LewRockwell.com*, and the author of *Yankee Wake Up* and *Free Your Inner Yankee*. He was a finalist for the 2010 Bastiat Prize for Online Journalism.

His popular writings have been published in dozens of media outlets ranging from *Forbes* to the *New York Post* to *American Banker* to regional newspapers, and his research has been profiled in dozens more, including *USA Today, Boston Globe, NPR, BBC, Guardian* (UK), *CNBC, Newsweek Poland, Financial Times Deutschland,* and others.

His research on behavioral and algorithmic finance has appeared in *Quantitative Finance, Journal of Wealth Management,* and *Risk and Decision Analysis,* among others, and his textbook *Financial Hacking* is due to be released by World Scientific in 2011.

I should disclose my own biases on this topic. I have described my philosophy as "Libertarian, but without the crazy stuff." Libertarians are for personal freedom, small government, and a defensive-sized military. That sounds good to me. But I think a better objective is something along the lines of maximizing the public's long term happiness. So while a libertarian might favor allowing his suburban neighbor to operate a bazooka firing range in his back yard, I'd be against that, even if it required a slightly larger government to prevent it.

Furthermore, I believe that if you identify with any political group or philosophy that has a name, you are far more susceptible to confirmation bias than someone who doesn't. And as a general rule, I don't trust anyone with a strong opinion on a complicated topic.

On the topic of the U.S. budget, my current suspicion is that the problem has grown so large that there is no practical way to eliminate the deficit by cuts alone, without making things worse. But I assure you that I want to be wrong because being right means my taxes will go up substantially.

Let's begin our interview.

Adams: Phil, thanks for agreeing to an interview with a professional humorist who holds an opposing viewpoint. I don't see how this could possibly go wrong for you. Let's start by setting the stage. In round numbers, what is the size of the total U.S. budget, and how large is the gap?

Maymin: The federal government spent $3.5 trillion of our money last year.

That's about the same as the total value of all the stocks in the Dow Jones Industrial Average. In other words, if we liquidated thirty of the largest American companies, including Home Depot, Microsoft, Intel, Coke, McDonald's, Kraft, and Disney, that would barely cover just one year of federal spending.

That's some budget.

Where did the feds get all that money? They took $2 trillion from us through taxes last year and they took another $1.5 trillion from us by borrowing on our good names. The "budget gap" is the $1.5 trillion that the government borrowed, adding to its $14 trillion debt. But in terms of the effect on the average person, borrowing money is the same as taxing.

Adams: Okay, so just to be clear, you're saying we need to find $1.5 trillion to cut from a budget of $3.5 trillion, for a 43% reduction. And that's just this year. Would it be fair to say government expenses will double in about twenty years as the baby boomers retire and healthcare costs continue their upward march?

Maymin: Government expenditures are not ruled by a fixed formula. You're tacitly assuming that the government is morally obligated to pay when people live too long or get too sick. But it's actually immoral to take money by force from innocent people to pay for someone else's retirement or someone else's sickness. Given your tacit assumption, then yes: government expenditures will continue to climb so long as people continue to vote for such immoral redistribution. But I don't agree with that assumption and, now that it is no longer tacit, I hope that neither do you.

Adams: We can get back to your hallucinations about my tacit assumptions later. For now I'm just trying to size the budget hole. Readers can't judge your recommended solution unless they have a sense of how big the problem is. Can we agree that balancing the budget would require cutting something like $1.5 trillion per year in the near term, while the demand for social services could double in twenty years, primarily because of an aging population, whether the government attempts to meet those needs or not?

Maymin: Your question about the "demand" for the future only makes sense if you view the federal government as a special charitable trust whose purpose is to pay a certain clearly defined group of people an amount of money based on its available funds.

But the federal government is not a charity. The main difference is that charities are funded by voluntary contributions, and the government is funded by forceful expropriation. So the self-regulating mechanism of a charity on the amount to pay out is broken. Indeed, instead of asking how much money we actually have, the government (and you) asks how much money we need to pay out. Aside from the immorality, the problem with that question is that the "demand" for free stuff is practically limitless. People could "demand" twice their benefits today. They don't necessarily have to wait for more people to retire or get sick.

But those "demands" aren't always met. There are forces resisting government redistribution. Will those forces be stronger or weaker in 20 years? Who knows? They will certainly need to become even stronger today if we want to not just freeze spending but actually cut it.

Adams: I'm using "demand" in the economic sense, i.e. hungry people have a demand for food. Demand doesn't imply that the government is the supplier.

I learned in business that unless you can describe what the business-as-usual scenario looks like, you have no way to compare your new and brilliant plan. I've asked you twice how large the future budget hole would get if left unaddressed and twice you have drifted into speeches about morality, complete with hallucinated assumptions about the question itself. So let's back up a step.

In general, do you think it's important to describe the economic impact of the "do nothing" or business-as-usual scenario so that one can judge the advantage of a new plan in comparison?

Maymin: Economic demand typically depends on price and assumes voluntary exchange. And of course your question implies the government is the supplier. That's the point of this discussion -- how to cut government spending. You're not asking about the demand for iPhones in 20 years.

For a legitimate business, sure, evaluating business-as-usual can be important, more important than some things, less important than others. But if your business is just going around breaking people's kneecaps, then no, you don't need to evaluate the economic impact of continuing. And what's the right response of the victim? To say, "Why don't you beat up this guy instead?" Or to say, "Stop."

I don't know how much politicians will redistribute income to retirees and sick people instead of wars and bailout in 20 years. But I know Americans would be better off if each of those four items were zero.

Adams: To borrow your analogy, if the only choices available are breaking your kneecaps or cutting off your head, it seems entirely legitimate to consider the kneecap option. Correct me if I'm misinterpreting your point, but you seem to believe the choices are something along the lines of the government breaking our kneecaps (the current approach) versus a world where the unemployable and sick eat carbon dioxide and poop hundred dollar bills.

Maybe I shouldn't put words in your mouth.

Perhaps we can get at this from another direction. In a world in which the budget is cut to your moral satisfaction, what becomes of the people who currently receive food, shelter and healthcare from the government?

Maymin: What happened to the East Germans who relied on the government when the wall fell? What would happen to North Koreans if that country becomes free? Ultimately voluntary help is always better than forced redistribution, but if we wait too long, the transition may be more abrupt than necessary. My suggestion would be to phase it out gradually while we still can.

Adams: I'm no historian, but I'm pretty sure the impoverished people from East Germany got help from the government of West Germany. And I'm pretty sure the poor in Germany still get help from the government.

So if I understand your concept, as the U.S. Government phases out social services, the government of Germany would pick up the slack.

I'm going to end the interview here. And I'll surprise you by showing some respect for your viewpoint. I wasn't expecting you to be such an absolutist on eliminating government spending for social services. It's entirely possible that private citizens would step up to take care of the needy, and perhaps do a better job of it than the government. And I can imagine a world in which I pay a little extra, voluntarily, to provide healthcare for my neighbor who is too sick to work. It might be a lot cheaper than paying taxes, while feeling less coercive and more meaningful. The Internet makes this sort of person-to-person helping possible whereas only the government could have done it fifty years ago.

We didn't discuss military spending, but I would respect any argument that ranges from a purely defensive military budget to something more aggressive "just in case." No one is smart enough to make that call.

Overall, I don't think Dr. Maymin's philosophy for government spending can be called a *plan* until someone can describe how the transition away from government social services is accomplished without clogging our streets with the corpses of the starved. But if I am fair about this, our government currently has a spending plan that guarantees doom. Advantage: Maymin.

Thanks for being a good sport, Dr. Maymin. And thanks for some ideas that add a lot to the discussion.

Originally published on February 11, 2011